HELLO, I'M JOHNNY CASH

★ ★ ★

G. NERI

ILLUSTRATED BY A. G. FORD

CANDLEWICK PRESS

I'M BOUND FOR THE PROMISED LAND

Before he became
Johnny Cash,
he was simply called
J.R. —
a name that stood for
nothing,
and nothing
was all he had
coming into this world.
By the time
he was three,
J.R.'s family
was close to ruin,
forced to flee
southern Arkansas
before the desperate winds
of the Great Depression
turned them all
to dust.
They hit the road
searching for a better life,
with nothing but the clothes
on their backs,
a few belongings,
and Momma's ol' beat-up
guitar.

It was on that bitterly
cold journey north
that J.R. sang his first
song.
Huddled
next to his brothers
and sisters
in the back of a
flatbed truck,
J.R. sang aloud,
his teeth clattering as
Momma beat out the gospels
on her guitar.
*I am bound
for the Promised Land!"*
they cried out,
the wind howling
all around them.

Scared and hungry,
J.R. asked, "Where
is the Promised Land,
Momma?"
She smiled and said,
"Two days north,
in a place called Dyess,"

where the mud
of the black delta land
was as thick as gumbo
and the promise
of the New Deal
as good as gold.

J.R. kept singing
that song
over and over,
hoping and praying
that promise
would come true.

"WHERE IS THE PROMISED LAND, MOMMA?"

FIVE FEET HIGH

Surrounded by a jungle
of thickets and boulders,
Dyess sure didn't look like
the Promised Land.
J.R. gazed out from
their bare-bones house
as Daddy, brother Roy,
and a stubborn mule
busted their backs
taming twenty acres
of New Deal land.
It would take months
of blood, sweat,
and tears
to turn that
tangled mess of
scrub oak

into fields of
prickly white
cotton.

It was a hard life.
Daddy, Momma,
and the older kids
were up at dawn
and spent all day in the fields
under the hot sun.
Hoeing, planting,
weeding, and picking
till their fingers bled—
the work never stopped.

His daddy was warned
from the get-go:
"Being a southern farmer

AND RISING

is like walking a tightrope—
one slip and
you're doomed."
To J.R.,
it seemed they were
always slipping—
fighting off deadly snakes
and wildcats,
battling to keep
the mighty Mississippi
from swallowing up their farm
in the Great Flood of '37,
losing entire crops
to seasons of drought and frost
or plagues of army worms
destroying everything
in their path.

It was tough on everyone—
things were there one day
and gone the next.

But Momma's guitar
was always there
to calm J.R.'s fears
with its comforting sounds,
until one day
that disappeared too—
sold
to buy food or clothing
because
music might feed
the soul
but couldn't feed
the family.

FAR AWAY PLACES

Too young
to work the fields,
J.R. watched
from the front porch
as his family
headed out to
the cotton patch.
He hated
being by himself,
so Daddy bought him
a small battery-powered radio
to keep him company.

From day one,
J.R. was glued
to that tiny speaker,
amazed
by the endless songs
playing just for him.
Beautiful music
came out of that box—
simple
but heavenly—
guitar, bass, drums,
and a voice.
Those radio stations
took him
to faraway places

like Nashville,
New Orleans,
or Del Rio, Texas,
playing songs
about a world
he'd never imagined
before.
Folk, blues, cowboy, gospel,
and pop music—
the radio had it all.
To Momma's surprise,
J.R. remembered
all the songs he heard.
He could sing
"Hobo Bill's Last Ride"
like Jimmie Rodgers himself.
Pretty soon
the neighbors took notice,
dropping by
to hear him belt out a tune
with his tiny voice—
J.R., the human radio
at just five years old.

At bedtime,
when Daddy told him
to go to sleep,
J.R. would press his ear

to the speaker
to catch the last few moments
of a world free
of cotton and mud.
He dreamed that
someday
he'd fly away
to those faraway places
and write songs about them
for the radio,
so that some kid
might hear them
and dream a little
too.

SOMEDAY
HE'D FLY
AWAY

FLESH AND BLOOD

Nobody was closer to J.R.
than his big brother
Jack Dempsey Cash.
He was only two years older,
but since J.R. was so
scrawny and shy,
Jack became his protector,
mentor, and best friend
all rolled into one.

Jack wasn't just strong
like the boxing champ
he was named after;
he was a deep thinker too.
Like their granddaddy
the horseback preacher,
he had the calling
to teach the Bible.
He taught J.R.
right from wrong
and about hard work
and sacrifice.
But he also knew
how to have fun.
Sharing secrets
at the fishing hole,
climbing trees
like squirrels,
or reading passages
from Jack's dog-eared
miniature Bible
late into the night—
the two were never
apart.

Jack was fearless.
When Daddy drank too much
and turned his anger
on Momma and the kids,
it was Jack
who stood up to him.
When J.R. found a stray dog
and Daddy shot it
because it killed
two of their chickens,
it was Jack who helped
ease his pain.

By the time J.R. was eight,
he and Jack were working
side by side
picking cotton with the rest
of the family
in the sweltering Arkansas heat.
As he pulled his cotton sack
along the darkened earth,
J.R. sang, lifting
everyone's spirits
with his high voice.
He sang novelty songs,
folk and pop songs,
and challenged his sister Louise
to hum any tune and he'd guess it.
J.R. knew them all.
By late afternoon,
when misery set in,
he turned to gospel,
stoking the last embers
of fire in their bellies,
so they could fill
their cotton sacks
one more time
before the skies
grew dark.

For a southern Baptist boy,
being saved
at a church revival
was a rite of passage—
the first step toward
accepting God
into your life.
But for J.R.,
sitting in those church pews
was terrifying—
all that shouting and crying,
gasping and praying.
They sure didn't act like
they were being saved
from the devil.
People broke out
in fevers and shakes
and threw their hands up
in the air
when the preacher yelled
"Repent! Or the wrath of God
will strike you down!"
J.R. would grab the pew
in front of him,
his knuckles turning
white with fear.
He was not without sin—
sometimes stealing cigarettes
and thinking bad thoughts—
and watching the sky
light up one night
from a nearby grass fire,
he felt like hell was
coming for him.

Music
was the only thing
that kept him going back.
He loved the gospels,
with those soaring voices
and angelic harmonies.
For Jack,
salvation meant
the Bible.
For J.R.,
it was all about
the music.

When he was twelve,
J.R. answered the call
to be saved.
The music was so powerful
it just made him stand up
and walk to the altar.
When the preacher laid his hand
on J.R.'s forehead,
a sense of peace
washed over him.
Afterward, he felt
even closer to Jack,
like somehow
they were equals now.
Before they were joined
by blood;
now they were
spiritual brothers
too.

I CAME TO BELIEVE

MEET ME IN HEAVEN

It started off
as a perfect spring day—
one of those Saturdays
where he and Jack
would laze about,
fishing under
the weeping willows
that lined
the Tyronza River.

J.R. wanted Jack
to come fishing,
like they did most Saturdays.
But times were tough,
and Jack had a chance
to earn some extra money
for the family.
Jack knew he should go to work,
but he kept stalling.
"I feel like something bad
is gonna happen," he said.
J.R. tried to get Jack
to change his mind
but couldn't stop him
from going.

Alone
at the fishing hole,
J.R. had a wretched feeling
in his gut all morning.
Hours later,
when a black car
headed his way,
J.R.'s heart
skipped a beat.
Daddy was
in the passenger seat.
"Leave the pole," he called out.
"Jack's been hurt really bad."

Daddy told him
that Jack had fallen
on a table saw
while cutting fence posts.
"I'm afraid
we're going to lose him."
It was the first time
J.R. saw his daddy
cry.

At the hospital,
the family gathered around,
praying and crying.
Jack opened his eyes
one last time.
"Can you hear
the angels singing?"
he said.
"I'm going there, Momma."

The day after
they lowered Jack's body
into the earth,
the family
had to work
the fields.
J.R. felt like he had died too.
He thought if only
he'd tried harder to stop Jack
from going to work,
he might've saved him.
Watching Momma
fall to her knees in the fields
with tears in her eyes
was almost too much
for him to bear.

J.R. didn't know
what to do,
so he just started singing
the spirituals from
Jack's funeral,
and Momma
stopped crying
to listen.
J.R. kept singing
all afternoon,
letting his pain
pour out through
his high strong voice,
which carried for miles
across the fields
to the heavens
above.

HURT

After Jack's death,
all J.R. talked about
was his brother.
But after a while,
his friends got tired
of hearing those stories,
so J.R. just stopped talking
about him altogether.

Instead, he'd walk
for miles
alone,
writing sad poems
in his head.
One day
J.R. found himself walking
down by the fishing hole.
He heard someone
playing a perfect rhythm
on the guitar
and thought maybe
it was a radio.
Turned out
it was
a crippled boy
playing in front of a
rundown shack.
J.R. had seen
other kids make fun
of this boy,
whose hand and foot

were deformed
by polio.
They laughed
and imitated the way
he limped into town.

But J.R. didn't care a lick.
That boy's music spoke
to him.
He was like
some kind of magician,
creating incredible sounds
with that withered right hand.

J.R. started dropping by
at the end of every day
to listen from
across the road.
After a few days,
the boy invited him over.
His name was Jesse Barnhill,
and he loved music
as much as J.R. did.
He taught J.R. his first chord
on the guitar.
Jesse understood
J.R.'s sad poems
and helped turn them
into songs.
They'd play late
into the nights,

and for J.R.,
it was pure heaven.
On his long walks home,
the wildcats growling
in the darkness,
J.R. sang out loud,
knowing the music
would protect him
from all that was
dark and scary
in the world.

One day J.R. said,
"You know, Jesse,
you've got polio,
but you sure can play."
Jesse just shrugged.
"Sometimes
when you lose a gift,
you get another one."

THE MUSIC WOULD PROTECT HIM

OH, WHAT A DREAM

The rest of the time,
J.R. could be found
hauling a six-foot cotton sack
through the fields.
Hard work helped
get his mind off Jack.
On some days,
he worked so hard,
he ended up with
300 pounds of cotton.
His one break in the day
was lunch,
but he usually had something
other than food
on his mind.
The *High Noon Roundup*
was the most talked about
radio show
in the Mid-South for one reason—
the Louvin Brothers.

Those country boys were
considered
the best duo ever,
and hearing them got J.R.
through many a day.
When he found out
they were coming
to perform at the local
high school,
J.R. knew he had to go.

He showed up two hours early,
and when the brothers finally
stepped onto the stage,
it was like they'd walked
right out of the radio
and into J.R.'s life.
He wanted to tell them,
"I'm going to be a singer
on the radio someday too!"
But the music
left him speechless.
Their rousing harmonies
pushed the crowd to their feet,
stomping with joy.
In person,
they were twice as good
as on the radio.

Sitting in the front row,
J.R. felt every note
washing over him—
he was never happier.
The pain and weariness
from Jack's passing lifted,
and after the show,
he floated

all the way home.
That night,
he couldn't sleep.
He'd seen the future—
it was a stage,
and he knew he belonged
on it.

Daddy thought that
big dreams were
a waste of time
for a country boy
"You'll never be anything
as long as you got that music
on your mind,"
he warned.

But J.R. couldn't help it—
he felt the music calling
like a voice
from the middle of the earth,
full of mystery
and power,
reaching up
and grabbing hold
of his heart.

His brother Roy,
who once dreamed of
being in a band of his own,
told him to follow his gut.
"Someday,
you're going to be
somebody.
The world's your apple,
and you're going to
peel it."

Even though Daddy
was against it,
Momma kept encouraging
J.R. to sing—
it was the only time
he seemed at peace
after Jack's passing.
She thought his music
brought him closer
to God,
so she pushed him
to perform in church,
where his strong tenor voice
rang out like
the gospel truth.
Folks listened eagerly,
as moved by his singing
as they had been
by the voice of his
granddaddy the preacher
long ago.

Momma wanted him
to take singing lessons,
thinking it might help
his chances to succeed.

She worked a whole day
doing other people's laundry
to pay for the lesson.
But when the teacher
asked J.R. to sing,
she was stunned
by the voice she heard.
"Don't ever
take voice lessons again,"
the teacher said.
"Don't let me
or anyone else
change the way
you sing."

One hot summer day,
after J.R.'s seventeenth birthday,
he and Daddy
chopped wood
for almost twelve hours
straight.
J.R. dragged himself home,
singing as he always did
after a hard day's work.
Momma turned around,
surprised.

"Who was that singing
in such a low, booming voice?"
"That was me," said J.R.
Her eyes filled
with tears. "You sound
exactly like your granddaddy."

J.R. shouted out,
"Hey, my voice dropped!"
He was startled
at how low he could sing.
His voice was suddenly
as smooth and deep
as the Mississippi itself.

Momma looked him
straight in the eye.
"God has His hand
on you, son,"
she said.
"You have the gift.
And you'll be singing
for the world
someday."

CAN'T HELP BUT WONDER
WHERE I'M BOUND

WE'LL MEET AGAIN

J.R.'s senior-class trip
gave him a taste
of life outside
Dyess.
Music City—
Nashville, Tennessee—
was like a dream to him.
He'd heard and read
so much about it,
that he couldn't sit still
for the entire 250 miles
they traveled.
Not only were they headed
for country's most famous stage,
the Grand Ole Opry,
but they would also be seeing
his favorite vocal group,
the Carter Family!

Momma used to sing
Carter Family songs
when J.R. was small
and he'd loved them ever since.
His favorite song,
"Can the Circle Be Unbroken,"
usually featured
their youngest member,

June Carter,
who was barely
older than him.
The first time
he ever heard her
cracking jokes
on the radio,
J.R. laughed
all day long.

When he finally saw June
in person
from the balcony
of the theater,
J.R. was smitten.
She was beautiful
and could sing
like nobody's business.
He was suddenly struck
with a feeling
that sooner or later
they'd be singing
together
on that very stage.

From then on,
he kept track

of her travels,
listening
as she popped up
on the radio
from all over
the country.
He knew someday
he'd catch up to her.
And the day he was singing
next to June Carter
would be the day
that he truly arrived.

SOONER OR LATER THEY'D BE SINGING TOGETHER

I'LL FLY AWAY

After high school,
Dyess no longer held much
for J.R.—
Jack was gone,
cotton was no longer king,
and jobs were scarce.
Once he tried to work
in the auto plants up North,
but he only lasted three weeks.
Being cooped up
on the assembly line
was too much
for a country boy.

Stuck back home,
J.R. dreamed of one day
flying out of
those cotton fields
into the wild blue
yonder.
Daddy had traveled
to all kinds of places
with the Army—
from New Mexico
to fight off Pancho Villa,
all the way to France
to battle the Germans
in World War I.
For J.R.,
the Air Force
would be his ticket out.
When the Korean War began,

he joined up,
giving himself the name
John R. Cash
because the military
required a full name
to enlist.

During boot camp,
his higher-ups discovered
he had a special talent.
They sent him to
faraway Germany,
where he found himself
listening to the radio
once again.
Only this time,
it was serious business—
top secret, in fact—
he was intercepting
coded messages
from the Russians.
All those years
of listening to every note
of every song
turned him into
a master radio operator.

John worked long hours,
and to pass the time,
he hummed along to the
beat and rhythm
of the Morse code

coming in over his headset.
He imagined Momma's
old guitar playing along too,
and suddenly
he knew what he needed
to overcome his homesickness.
John trudged
through miles of blizzard
to find what he was looking for—
a cheap five-dollar guitar.
He hugged it to his body
and felt the warmth
of the music
it would bring.

He remembered the few chords
that Jesse had taught him
and started playing.
The sound of that guitar
soon pulled in
a few other
lonely country boys
from the base.
They formed a band
called the Barbarians—
because that's what
their music sounded like
to the Germans.
But it didn't matter
that they weren't any good.
To John,
playing together
transported him
from those bitterly
cold nights
to a warm summer's day
way back home.

I'M GOING TO MEMPHIS

After four years away,
Staff Sergeant Cash
came back to America
a man.
The first thing he did
was marry a young woman
who had literally knocked him
off his feet—
in a roller-skating rink
back in Texas,
where he'd gone to boot camp.
John had written
Vivian Liberto
the whole time he was
away,
the two of them
falling in love
by air mail.
Reunited at last,
they headed to Memphis,
the place that was about to
change music
forever.

Needing money
to start a family,
John got a job
selling refrigerators
door-to-door,
but his heart
just wasn't in it.

He spent most of his time
dreaming
and listening to
the car radio.
"You're the worst salesman
I've ever seen," said his boss.
But he knew John had
bigger ambitions
than selling appliances.
John had his heart set
on his music,
so his boss lent him money
to pursue his dream.
John was thankful. "Someday
I'm gonna come back
and repay you in full,"
he promised.

One day, John heard a
boom-chicka-boom sound
coming from the back
of the auto shop
where his brother Roy worked.
It reminded him of the trains
that used to rattle
their childhood home.
Some mechanic friends of Roy's—
Luther and Marshall—
were messing around
on a guitar and a bass.
John fell in with them,

three dreamers
in love with music.
That train sound
put them on a track,
not to the local clubs,
where they were turned away
for playing hillbilly music,
but to church,
where they were invited
to sing one Sunday night.
They had no suits,
and the only matching clothes
they had were
black.
"Black will be better
for church anyways," John said.

They walked up to the altar
with their beat-up speakers and
hand-me-down instruments.
But the audience didn't care,
because as soon as
John opened his mouth,
it was like hearing
the voice of God
backed by bass and guitars.
After that,
John started wearing black
all the time.

GET RHYTHM

John was on his way
to the grand opening of
a new store in town
when he heard
screaming.
He rushed to see
what all the commotion
was about, and
when he turned the corner,
he couldn't believe his eyes.
Elvis Presley
wasn't just singing
on the back of a flatbed truck;
he was gyrating
like a tornado,
whipping
three hundred girls
into a frenzy
with his music.
John had never seen
anything like it.
That should be me!
he thought jealously.

Later,
John sought out Elvis
and was surprised to find
a soft-spoken country boy

just like himself—
with a love of gospel music
to boot.
Soon they were trading licks
on guitar.
"Say, whaddya call
that music
you were playing?" asked John.
"Rock and roll," said Elvis.
He and his producer,
Sam Phillips,
both loved the beat of the blues
and the soul of country music.
They mixed it all together
and came up with
a new sound.
John wanted some of that
magic.

Soon after,
John started showing up
at Sun Records,
where he pestered Sam Phillips
into listening to him sing.
For two hours,
John sang
every country and gospel tune
he knew from the radio.

Unimpressed,
Sam said, "Sing something
you wrote."
John remembered
a song he had written
while waiting for the train
to bring him home
from the Air Force.
When he let loose
with "Hey, Porter,"
Sam was moved.
That deep thunder
of his voice and the ache
in his lyrics
made the song
believable and true.
"That's the one! That's
going to be a record,"
said Sam.

John only had a few cents
left to his name,
but afterward
he was so happy
that when a panhandler
stuck out his hand,
John gave him all he had.

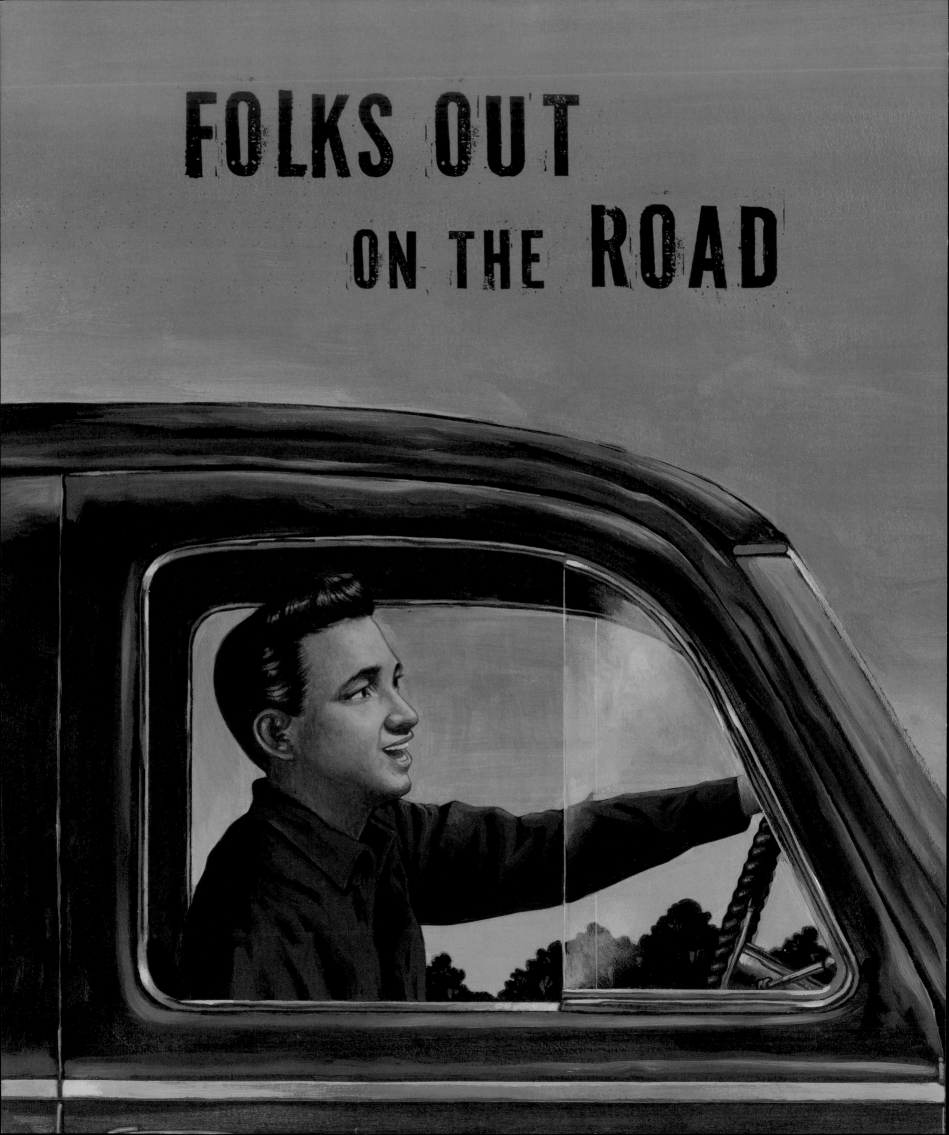

It had been quite a year
since John returned
from Germany.
Here he was,
not only about to become
a real singer,
but a *dad* as well.
A month before
his first record came out,
Vivian gave birth
to their first daughter,
Rosanne.
Strumming lullabies
to his baby at night,
John felt like
maybe God did have
His hand on him.

A few weeks later,
he was driving on the highway,
when "Hey, Porter"
came on the radio.
He almost drove off the road.
John couldn't believe
that was his voice
going out over
the airwaves.
He thought about
all the songs
he'd heard on the radio
that had given him hope,

calmed his despair,
or just let him escape
his troubles
for a few moments.
He looked at the cars around him
and wondered if maybe
they were listening
to that same station
and finding strength
and inspiration
through his music now.

His first royalty check
came in for $6.42.
It wasn't much,
but he felt like
the richest man
in town.
When fan mail
started to trickle in,
John would lay
the letters out on the floor
and marvel
at all the different states
they came from.
What a world
he lived in—
singing
and getting paid for it
too!

I WALK THE LINE

Sam thought John needed
a little extra flash,
so he started calling him
Johnny,
and the name stuck.
Marshall and Luther
became his band—
the Tennessee Two—
driving that
boom-chicka-boom sound
behind all his songs.

At his first big show,
opening for Elvis,
Johnny Cash stood out
from the get-go.
He didn't sing that
sugary country music
like the guys who wore
glittery cowboy outfits.
He wore black,
and his voice had a raw power
that penetrated the heart
of anyone who heard it.
That night,
all of Johnny's family
and friends

watched as he set the stage
on fire with an energy
that left the crowd hungry
for more.
The audience
kept calling him back
for an encore,
and after singing
his two songs again and again,
he finally broke out a new one,
"Folsom Prison Blues."
The crowd went
crazy for it.

Johnny was overwhelmed.
Afterward,
one of his radio heroes,
Sonny James,
took him aside.
"Looks like you got it made.
But remember,
what you are
and the life you live
sings louder than any song."

Johnny never forgot that.
It made him want

to write a song
about who he was
and how he wanted to live
his life.
The song would be
a vow to stay true
to his heart
and to the family
he loved.

The words just poured out.
In twenty minutes,
Johnny Cash had written
the biggest song
of his life.
When "I Walk the Line"
became the number-one
country song in America,
Johnny went back to the boss
who had lent him money
to pursue his dreams
and paid him back in full.

"WHAT YOU ARE AND THE LIFE YOU LIVE SINGS LOUDER THAN ANY SONG."

"HELLO, I'M JOHNNY CASH"

is how he started
every concert from then on.
That simple statement
said it all.

Johnny Cash,
the poor country boy
from the cotton fields,
traveled the world
many times over,
where he sang
for presidents
and the homeless,
businessmen and farmers,
soldiers and prisoners alike.
It didn't matter how famous he got;
he never forgot
what it felt like to be cold,
miserable, and hungry.
Momma didn't have to
remind Johnny
that his gift was special.
He knew he was not its owner
but its caretaker.

"I'll always be true to it,"
he promised her.

Being true meant
being unafraid to speak
from the heart.
Just as Jack had believed in
right from wrong,
the Man in Black believed
his role was to sing the truth,
whether it was popular or not.
His songs gave a voice
to the voiceless,
capturing so many people's
heartaches, struggles, and triumphs,
it seemed like he spoke
for America
just as America spoke
to him.

For almost forty years,
he criss-crossed
this great land
as his concerts took him
down every major highway
to cities big and small.
But it was only after
he'd written a thousand songs,
sung ten thousand shows,
and sold over
fifty million records

that Johnny Cash
came to believe
that the Promised Land
was not a place
in Dyess, Arkansas,
or Landsberg, Germany,
or Memphis, Tennessee.
It was the feeling
he got in his heart
every time
he shared
his gift.

THE MAN IN BLACK

MORE ABOUT JOHNNY CASH ★ ★ ★

Johnny Cash (1932–2003) was one of the great voices of twentieth-century America. To many, he *was* America: salt of the earth, honest, kind to a fault, funny as heck, deeply religious, and deeply flawed. His rags-to-riches story is the essence of the American Dream, filled with promise, failure, and redemption.

Known as the Man in Black, Johnny had a deep bass voice that was instantly recognizable. He wrote more than 1,100 songs, recorded forty-five albums, had forty-eight singles in the Top 100, and won twelve Grammy Awards. He performed hundreds of shows a year for over thirty-eight years and sold well over fifty million records.

The *boom-chicka-boom* sound of Johnny's first record came about when Luther Perkins removed the metal plate from his guitar and muted the strings because he was embarrassed by his poor playing skills. Since they didn't have a drummer, Johnny wound some paper between the strings of his guitar, which made it sound more like a drum. Sam Phillips added some echo for effect but otherwise kept it simple: he didn't want anything distracting from Johnny's voice. In a time of polished studio recordings, Johnny Cash and the Tennessee Two's raw music was a revelation. Their first song, "Hey, Porter," went to number one in Memphis and number fourteen in the nation. It wasn't until 1960 that they added drummer W.S. Holland to make them the Tennessee Three.

On his first tour, Johnny joined the other Sun Records stars: Elvis Presley, Jerry Lee Lewis, and Carl Perkins. The press called them the Million Dollar Quartet. Their songs "I Walk the Line," "Heartbreak Hotel," "Great Balls of Fire," and "Blue Suede Shoes" defined a new sound that changed music forever. "I Walk the Line" became Johnny's biggest hit, topping the country music charts for forty-three weeks.

In 1969, with his ground-breaking hit albums *Johnny Cash at Folsom Prison* and *Johnny Cash at San Quentin,* he sold more records than the Beatles. These albums, recorded live in prisons, went against everything record companies thought would sell. The second album produced one of his biggest hits, "A Boy Named Sue," written by children's author Shel Silverstein.

At forty-eight, Johnny Cash was the youngest person ever to be chosen for the Country Music Hall of Fame, and he's one of just a few artists to have been selected for both the Country *and* Rock Music Halls of Fame. Toward the end of his career, Johnny Cash received the nation's top artistic honors: the Kennedy Center Honors and the National Medal of Arts.

Having fallen into "has-been" status by the 1980s, he was rediscovered, first by the mega-band U2 and then by producer Rick Rubin, who set him on a path to one of the greatest come-backs in modern music history. A whole new audience discovered Cash's music, and Country Music Television named him the Number One Country Artist of All Time.

For Johnny, the biggest prize of all was June Carter. Back in 1956, six years after he first saw her sing at the Grand Ole Opry, Johnny found himself backstage with June. Taken with the moment, he boldly told her, "You and I are going to get married someday." Though they were both married to other people at the time, Johnny and June later came together and proved to be a perfect match in both music and life. Her song "Ring of Fire" captured their burning love for each other and became a huge hit when Johnny sang it backed by mariachi trumpets. She helped him overcome his drug and alcohol addictions, which developed during endless months of performing on the road, and their unconditional love turned into one of the most celebrated marriages in all of country music.

Johnny and June performed together until she unexpectedly passed away in 2003. Johnny died four months later, at age seventy-one, of complications from diabetes and a broken heart. Johnny left behind four daughters and one son from his two marriages: Rosanne, Kathy, Cindy, Tara, and John. Rosanne became a country music star in her own right, and John became a music producer who helped record his parents' last albums, which garnered five Grammy Awards. Of Johnny's siblings—Roy, Louise, Jack, Reba, Joanne, and Tommy—only the latter two are alive as of this publication, both still touring as singers.

Johnny Cash recorded over thirty songs in the final few months of his life. The last recording was his version of a Carter Family staple called "Engine 143." From the unique *boom-chicka-boom* sound of his Sun Records days to his final sessions alone with a guitar in his log cabin, Johnny Cash's songs were all about the choices people made in their struggle between darkness and light, good and evil. He often said, "You can choose love or hate. Choose love." The gift of his voice and the love he spread through his singing will live forever.

★★★ HISTORICAL EVENTS IN JOHNNY'S LIFETIME

THE GREAT DEPRESSION (1929–1939): The longest period of economic hardship in American history began with the great stock market crash of '29, when banks closed and many people lost everything. By the time J.R. was born, the Great Depression affected nearly everyone in America, but southern farmers were hit the hardest. They were barely making it when times were good; now it was a disaster. One of Johnny's last albums, *My Mother's Hymn Book*, captures many of the gospel songs he sang with his mother during this difficult period.

THE NEW DEAL (1933–1936): President Franklin D. Roosevelt created a series of social programs as an answer to the Great Depression. When he was three, J.R.'s family moved from Kingsland to Dyess, Arkansas, a farming collective created under the New Deal that saved many from ruin. They became cotton farmers—a tough life, but they managed. Songs like "Pickin' Time" captured the hardships Johnny's family experienced while waiting for cotton-picking time—the only time they were ever paid. In later years, Johnny kept a cotton boll in a safe as a reminder of where he came from and how much he'd been blessed.

THE GOLDEN AGE OF RADIO (1930s–1940s): During the Great Depression, a radio was one of the few luxuries that many families had. Music, variety shows, and dramas became a welcome escape from these desperate times. By the mid-thirties, more than 22 million homes had radios, and cars were being sold with radios too. J.R.'s favorite show was the *High Noon Roundup*, which featured such stars as Eddie Hill, the Louvin Brothers, Hank Snow, Sonny James, Ernest Tubb, and the Carter Family.

THE GREAT FLOOD OF '37: In 1937, the Big Muddy—the Mississippi River—rose until it breached the levees and flooded most of the Arkansas Delta area. J.R. and his family evacuated, except for his father, who stayed until the water rose five feet. "Five Feet High and Rising" recounts J.R.'s experience escaping the flood on a raft made from a door. When they returned, there were snakes in the rafters and hens on the couch.

THE COLD WAR (1945–1990): Following World War II, the Soviet Union and the United States fell into a stalemate of aggression. Private John R. Cash was sent to Landsberg, Germany, where he became a radio operator, or "ditty bop," so named because they spent all their time chasing the dots and dashes of Morse code. He received a Presidential Commendation for locating the signal of the first Soviet jet bomber flying out of Moscow. He was also the first Westerner to discover that Soviet dictator Joseph Stalin had died. Johnny wrote one of his first hits, "Folsom Prison Blues," after seeing a movie in Landsberg about the famous prison.

THE BIRTH OF ROCK 'N' ROLL (1951–1955): Perhaps no other music shook youth culture worldwide like rock 'n' roll. The combining of rhythm and blues with country and hillbilly music started at Sun Records. In 1951, Sam Phillips recorded what is arguably the first rock-and-roll song—"Rocket 88" by Ike Turner, a black singer. By 1954, he was able to transform that black sound for white folks, through the likes of Elvis Presley, Jerry Lee Lewis, Roy Orbison, Carl Perkins, and Johnny Cash.

THE 1960s: This was a decade of tumultuous change—socially, politically, and culturally. The Vietnam War raged on, women and blacks fought for their civil rights, and music was turned on its head. Bob Dylan led the way with his protest songs against the injustices of the day. Johnny's prison albums and his concept album about the plight of the American Indians, with songs like "The Ballad of Ira Hayes," were his way of speaking out.

TELEVISION: In 1969, Johnny started a nationwide television broadcast called *The Johnny Cash Show*. He used this platform to bring controversial artists like Dylan, Joni Mitchell, Neil Young, Pete Seeger, and others to a new audience. The show was bold for its time, and he did it all from Middle America—Nashville, Tennessee. It reached audiences of all kinds: old and young, black and white, rich and poor. Despite being extremely popular, the show was cancelled in 1971 because Johnny refused to give in to sponsors who didn't like some of his outspoken guests. His song "The Man in Black," which outlined his political views, was first heard on this show.

POLITICS: Johnny personally knew every president from Nixon to George W. Bush, but was closest to June's distant cousin, Jimmy Carter. Johnny was a veteran and a patriot, entertaining soldiers in the field and acting as Grand Marshall in the national Bicentennial parade. But he wasn't afraid to speak his mind, calling for troop withdrawals in war protests, attending the Watergate hearings, and fighting every day to make his country a better place to live.

DISCOGRAPHY ★ ★ ★

It would take an entire book to list all of Johnny's recordings and compilations. Here are some suggestions for those looking for a place to start exploring his music:

- Compilations: *The Essential Johnny Cash* (2002), *Love, God, Murder* (2000), and *Cash Unearthed* (2003). A great overview of his entire body of work, from hits to rare outtakes.
- *Johnny Cash with His Hot and Blue Guitar* (1957). His first album, containing many of his great Sun recordings.
- *The Fabulous Johnny Cash* (1958). His first record without Sam Phillips, and one of his finest.
- *Ride This Train* (1960), *Blood, Sweat and Tears* (1963), and *Bitter Tears* (1964). Johnny broke away from mainstream country for several concept records that explored America's past, both glorious and troubled.
- *Johnny Cash at Folsom Prison* (1968) and *Johnny Cash at San Quentin* (1969). Two of the best live albums ever recorded and Johnny's biggest hits.
- The supergroups: *Highwayman* (1985), *Class of '55* (1986), and *Million Dollar Quartet* (1990). Johnny formed bands with some of the best country and rock 'n' roll singers ever.
- *American Recordings* (1994), *Unchained* (1996), and *American III–VI* (2000–2010). Johnny's epic collaboration with producer Rick Rubin led to one of the greatest comebacks of all time, cementing Johnny's legendary status as the elder statesman of cool.

While much has been written about the life of Johnny Cash, I deliberately set out to tell his story the way Johnny saw it. Every event that is mentioned in this book originated from his own words, either spoken or written. Where possible, I used dialogue approximating how he remembered it. Other times, I filled in the gaps inspired by the spirit of his recollections. These collected accounts were gathered from the following sources:

Cash, Johnny. *Man in Black.* Grand Rapids, MI: Zondervan, 1975.

———. *American Recordings,* album notes. Burbank, CA: Sony, 1994.

———. *Cash: The Autobiography.* San Francisco: Harper Collins, 1997.

———. *Cash Unearthed,* album notes. Burbank, CA: American Recordings/Lost Highway, 2003.

Cash, John Carter. *House of Cash: The Legacies of My Father, Johnny Cash.* San Rafael, CA: Insight Editions, 2011.

Dolan, Sean. *Johnny Cash.* New York: Chelsea House, 1995.

Elfstrom, Robert. *Johnny Cash: The Man, His World, His Music,* DVD. Cherry Red Studio, 2000.

Fine, Jason, ed. *Cash.* New York: Crown, 2004.

Miller, Bill. *Cash: An American Man.* New York: Pocket Books/Simon & Schuster, 2004.

Streissguth, Michael. *Ring of Fire: The Johnny Cash Reader.* Cambridge, MA: Da Capo, 2002.

Turner, Steve. *The Man Called Cash.* Nashville: W Publishing Group, 2004.

Waddell, Hugh, ed. *I Still Miss Someone: Friends and Family Members Remember Johnny Cash.* Nashville: Cumberland House, 2004.

★ ★ ★

BIBLIOGRAPHY

For my mom, who, like J.R.'s, was always there for me,
never doubting that I'd find my way
G. N.

To all musicians who aspire to create heartfelt
and honest music for our world
A. G. F.

Text copyright © 2014 by G. Neri
Illustrations copyright © 2014 by A. G. Ford

First edition 2014

Library of Congress Catalog Card Number 2013955685
ISBN 978-0-7636-6245-5

14 15 16 17 18 19 TTP 10 9 8 7 6 5 4 3 2 1

Printed in Huizhou, Guangdong, China

This book was typeset in Futura Book.
The illustrations were done in oil.

Candlewick Press
99 Dover Street
Somerville, Massachusetts 02144

visit us at www.candlewick.com